Audition Songs for Female Singers 3

Memory...

plus nine more essential audition standards

Wise Publications
London/New York/Paris/Sydney/Copenhagen/Madrid

Other titles in this series...

Audition Songs for Female Singers 1

Don't Cry For Me Argentina...

plus Adelaide's Lament, Big Spender; Heaven Help My Heart;
I Cain't Say No; I Will Survive; Out Here On My Own; Saving All My Love For You;
Someone To Watch Over Me; The Wind Beneath My Wings. ORDER NO. AM92587

Audition Songs for Female Singers 2

I Dreamed A Dream...

plus Another Suitcase In Another Hall; Fame; If I Were A Bell; Miss Byrd;
Save The Best For Last; Someone Else's Story; There Are Worse Things I Could Do;
What I Did For Love; You Can Always Count On Me. ORDER NO. AM950224

Audition Songs for Female Singers 4

I Don't Know How To Love Him...

plus As Long As He Needs Me; Constant Craving;
Feeling Good; I Say A Little Prayer; If My Friends Could See Me Now; It's Oh So Quiet;
Killing Me Softly With His Song; Tell Me It's Not True; You Must Love Me. ORDER NO. AM955295

Audition Songs for Male Singers 1

Tonight...

plus All Good Gifts; Anthem; Being Alive; Corner Of The Sky; Funny;
High Flying, Adored; If I Loved You; Luck Be A Lady; Why, God, Why? ORDER NO. AM92586

Audition Songs for Male Singers 2

Maria...

plus All I Need Is The Girl; Bring Him Home; Frederick's Aria;
I Don't Remember Christmas; Sit Down, You're Rocking The Boat; Some Enchanted Evening;
This Is The Moment; Where I Want To Be; You're Nothing Without Me. ORDER NO. AM950213

Exclusive Distributors:
Music Sales Limited
8/9 Frith Street,
London W1V 5TZ, England.
Music Sales Pty Limited
120 Rothschild Avenue,
Rosebery, NSW 2018,
Australia.

Order No. AM955284
ISBN 0-7119-7455-1
This book © Copyright 1999 by Wise Publications

Compiled by Paul Honey and Nick Crispin
Music arrangements by Paul Honey
Music processed by Enigma Music Production Services

CD performed and recorded by Paul Honey

Book design by Studio Twenty, London

Your Guarantee of Quality
As publishers, we strive to produce every book
to the highest commercial standards.
The music has been freshly engraved and the book has been
carefully designed to minimise awkward page turns and
to make playing from it a real pleasure.
Particular care has been given to specifying acid-free,
neutral-sized paper made from pulps which have not been
elemental chlorine bleached. This pulp is from farmed sustainable
forests and was produced with special regard for the environment.
Throughout, the printing and binding have been planned to ensure a
sturdy, attractive publication which should give years of enjoyment.
If your copy fails to meet our high standards, please inform us and
we will gladly replace it.

Music Sales' complete catalogue describes thousands of
titles and is available in full colour sections by subject, direct
from Music Sales Limited. Please state your areas of interest and
send a cheque/postal order for £1.50 for postage to:
Music Sales Limited, Newmarket Road, Bury St. Edmunds,
Suffolk IP33 3YB.

CD Track 1
Can't Help Lovin' Dat Man
Music: Page 4

CD Track 2
Crazy
Music: Page 8

CD Track 3
Diamonds Are A Girl's Best Friend
Music: Page 12

CD Track 4
Now That I've Seen Her
Music: Page 15

CD Track 5
Memory
Music: Page 20

CD Track 6
Show Me Heaven
Music: Page 26

CD Track 7
That Ole Devil Called Love
Music: Page 30

CD Track 8
The Winner Takes It All
Music: Page 34

CD Track 9
Wishing You Were Somehow Here Again
Music: Page 40

CD Track 10
The Reason
Music: Page 44

Can't Help Lovin' Dat Man

Music by Jerome Kern
Words by Oscar Hammerstein II

Medium swing

Oh lis-ten sis-ter, I love my Mis-ter

man____ and I can't__ tell yo' why,__ Dere ain't no rea-son

why I should love dat man.

It must be sump-in' dat de an-gels done plan.

Fish got to swim, birds got to fly, I got to love one

man till I die, Can't help lov-in' dat man of

And when he comes back dat day is fine,___ The sun will shine.

He can come home___ as late as can be,___ Home with-out him___ ain't

no home to me,___ Can't help lov - in' dat man___ of

1. mine.___ **2.** mine.

Crazy

Words & Music by Willie Nelson

Diamonds Are A Girl's Best Friend

Words by Leo Robin
Music by Jule Styne

Bright swing

kiss may be grand but it won't pay the ren- tal on your
may come a time when a hard- boiled em- ploy- er thinks you're

hum- ble flat, or help you at the Au- to- mat.
aw- ful nice, but get that "ice" or else no dice.

Men grow cold as girls grow old, and we
He's your guy as when stocks grow are high, but be-

all lose our charms in the end. But
-ware when they start to de- scend. It's

Now That I've Seen Her (Her Or Me)

Music by Claude-Michel Schönberg
Lyrics by Richard Maltby Jr. & Alain Boublil

Moderato

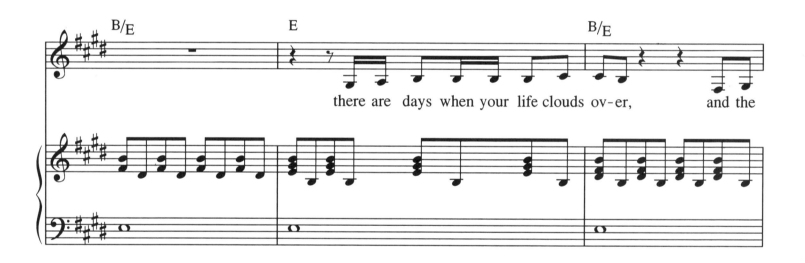

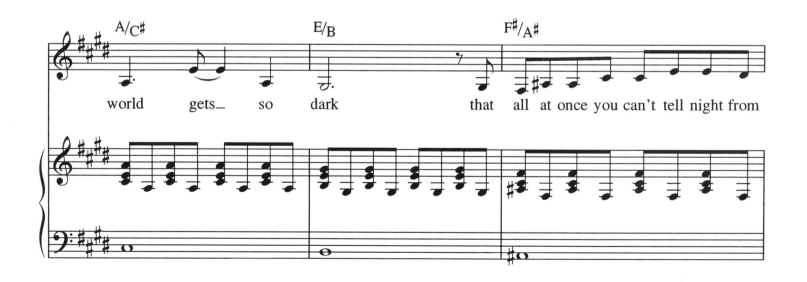

hide, she is not some fling____ from long a-go.___ Now that__ I've

seen her__ I know why__ he lied, and I think it was

bet-ter when I did-n't know._____

In her eyes, in her voice,

Memory

Music by Andrew Lloyd Webber
Text by Trevor Nunn after T.S. Eliot

me - - mory_____ live___ a - gain.

poco più mosso

Ev - 'ry street lamp seems to beat_____ a

fa - tal - is - - tic war - - ning.

Some - one mut - ters___ and a street lamp gut - ters___ and

21

soon it will be morn - - ing.

Tempo I

Day - light.___ I must wait for the sun - - rise,___ I must think of a

new life___ And I must-n't give in. When the

dawn comes to-night will be a me - mo - ry too___ And a

new day____ will__ be - gin.

leave me____ All a-lone with the me - m'ry____ Of my days in the

sun._____ If you touch me you'll un - der - stand what

hap-pi ness is. Look a new day has be - gun.

Show Me Heaven

Words & Music by Maria McKee, Jay Rifkin & Eric Rackim

1. There you go, flash-ing fe-ver from your eyes.—
(Verse 2 see block lyric)

Hey babe,— come ov - er here— and shut down tight.—

I'm not de ny - ing we're fly-ing a-bove— it all,—

Verse 2:
Here I go, I'm shaking just like the breeze.
Hey babe, I need your hand to steady me.
I'm not denying I'm frightened as much as you.
Though I'm barely touching you,
I've shivers down my spine, and it feels divine.

Oh, show me heaven, *etc.*

That Ole Devil Called Love

Words & Music by Doris Fisher & Allan Roberts

The Winner Takes It All

Words & Music by Benny Andersson & Bjorn Ulvaeus

Rhythmically

talk   a - bout things we've gone through,
2. arms   think -ing I   be -longed there,
(Verses 3 & 4 see block lyric)

though it's hurt-ing   me,   now it's his -to-
I   fi - gured it   made sense,   build-ing me   a

ry.   I've played all   my cards
fence,   build - ing   me   a   home,

and that's what you've done   too,   no -thing more to
think-ing   I'd   be   strong there,   but   I   was   a

CODA

The win-ner takes it all.

Verse 3:

But tell me, does she kiss like I used to kiss you,
Does it feel the same when she calls your name?
Somewhere deep inside,
You must know I miss you,
But what can I say,
Rules must be obeyed.
The judges will decide the likes of me abide,
Spectators of the show always staying low.

Verse 4:

I don't wanna talk
If it makes you feel sad
And I understand you've come to shake my hand.
I apologise if it makes you feel bad
Seeing me so tense,
No self-confidence.
The winner takes it all.
The winner takes it all.

Wishing You Were Somehow Here Again

Music by Andrew Lloyd Webber
Lyrics by Charles Hart. Additional lyrics by Richard Stilgoe

The Reason

Words & Music by Carole King, Mark Hudson & Greg Wells

son.___ you are the rea - son__ I wake up ev-'ry day__ and sleep__

through the night,__ you are the rea - son,__ the rea - - son.

In the mid - dle of the night I'm go-ing down__ 'cause {I a -
'cause {I__

dore___you,} I want__ to floor you.__ I'm giv-ing it up__
want___you,}

rea - - son, you are the rea- rea - - son.

The rea - - son._____

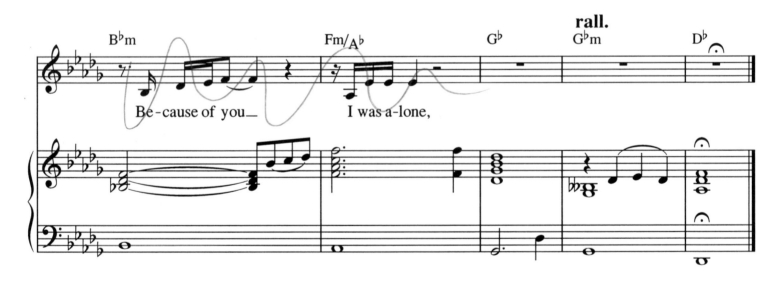

Be-cause of you___ I was a-lone,

Verse 2:
I'm giving it up
No more running around spinning my wheel
You came out of my dream and made it real
I know what I feel, it's you,
It's all because of you.

8/00 (37826)